SHOOTING STARS

Shooting Stars

CHAMPIONSHIP ARCHERY TECHNIQUES

**Compiled by
John Holden**

The Crowood Press

First published in 1987 by
The Crowood Press
Ramsbury, Marlborough
Wiltshire SN8 2HE

British Library Cataloguing in Publication Data

Shooting stars : championship archery
   techniques.
   1. Archery
   I. Holden, John, *1947–*
   799.3′2   GV1185
   ISBN 1 85223 006 1

Illustrations by John Holden

Typeset by Inforum, Portsmouth
Printed in Great Britain at the University Printing House, Oxford

Contents

Preface

Only a tiny minority of tournament archers succeed in breaking the 1250 FITA barrier. Mostly, their careers are brief: literally here one season, gone the next. Only a few champions maintain their performance consistently enough to become established in their national team and on the world circuit. Currently, the only British male FITA target archers to hold that exalted position are Mark Blenkarne and Steve Hallard.

What does it take to shoot so predictably well? This and a thousand more questions buzz through the minds of less able shooters and the coaching fraternity. Theory, supposition, fact and fancy abound. 'Ah, yes,' you'll hear somebody say, 'But those lads shoot all day, every day. They get dozens of free bows to try. And they won't ever tell you about their secret methods.'

When Blenkarne and Hallard shoot arrow after arrow with machine-like technique and accuracy, are you seeing a demonstration of talent pure and simple, or even the result of knowledge deliberately denied to archers in general? Their success is a direct result of determination and sheer hard work. In fact, they are compelled to struggle under an unfair burden: while the rest of the world's top archers are professionals in all but name, the British pair are strictly amateur.

It seemed to me that the logical way to discover their 'secrets' was to ask them, but would they be willing to explain and demonstrate? 'Yes, of course,' they said, surprised that anybody should have thought otherwise. This book is the result. In their own words backed up by picture sequences, Mark and Steve go through their techniques, training schedules and equipment to reveal the important mechanical aspects of form and control, and to explain how these are reinforced by fitness exercises and mental conditioning to produce the flowing, effortless control and confidence that overpowers the opposition.

The third member of the trio, Philip van Buren, introduces compound bow shooting. Still controversial but growing in stature, the target compound attracts more enthusiasts every season, some from the recurve ranks and others who were drawn into archery by the aura of technology that surrounds eccentric wheels, telescopic sights and release aids. A Master Bowman in field and target disciplines, coach and dealer, Philip blends shooting ability with the necessary experience of the bow's technical design, tuning and selection.

JOHN HOLDEN
February 1987

Mark Blenkarne

MY ARCHERY CAREER

My archery career began in 1967 as a result of picking up a copy of *Archery – Know the Game* in a local sports shop. At school I had not been particularly interested in sport and disliked the normal team games, but I thought that archery sounded interesting. Bristol Bowmen, the local club, was about a mile from my home, so I wrote to the secretary asking if they ran beginner's courses. To my disappointment, the club did not permit children under twelve to shoot, but if I wanted to go to the ground they would assess if I was sensible enough to be an exception to the rule. Luckily they approved of me, and I joined. Over the next few years I shot three times a week and enjoyed it. After about three years, a junior older than I joined the club and started a battle between us. We both increased our performance out of all recognition as we continually fought to beat each other.

I won the Silver Medal in the Under 16s National Championships and progressed gradually until 1975 when I won the National Junior Championships. The following year I won the National Senior Championships, principally because the top two archers were at the Olympics at the time. 1977 saw my first British Team appearance at the Nations Tournament in Hanover, West Germany. Not until 1978 did I get a place in the full team competing for the European Championships held that year in Coventry, England. With only a month to go, I was not shooting very well and asked Gary Sykes to coach me. After intensive training I managed to shoot well in the tournament, achieving sixth place individually. The British men's team came third overall; an immensely satisfying result, particularly as the tournament was held on British soil.

The next two years were probably my most successful. I won a FITA Star tournament in Strasbourg, France, with a new British record of 1257. Next, we were off to the World Championships in Berlin – an enjoyable trip because the British Army looked after us so well, even placing a minibus and driver at our disposal. The whole team shot well, and the ladies won the Bronze Team Medal. I finished sixth overall and won the 70m Medal, beating Darrell Pace and Rick McKinney at that distance.

During the winter of 1979–80 I trained harder than I had ever done before and approached the new season very positively. I have always found that the fitter I am physically, the better and more positive is my mental approach. There were only three tournaments before a team was selected for the Olympic Games to be held in Moscow. I was absent from one of them while competing in a multi-nation event in Romania where I had my first taste of standing on top of the podium with the national anthem playing. I had shot well, breaking the British double FITA round record. Principally because of this, I was selected for Moscow.

It was unfortunate that a great deal of political controversy affected the tournament, but once shooting was under way that did not seem to matter so much. At times I managed to climb to the top of the leader board, but finally slipped a couple of places to finish just outside the medals in fourth position. On returning to Britain, I competed in the British Championships where I achieved a good performance of two 1100 Yorks, and my third championship title in a row. By 1982 I had made it five wins in a row.

The 1980 European Championships were a disappointment for me personally as I finished in a lowly 27th spot, possibly because I had shot myself out at the British Championships. I felt that I had peaked at that point, and in hindsight perhaps I should have missed the tournament. At the time, however, I wanted to complete a hat trick of British Target Championships.

My degree finals prevented me

Fig 1

Fig 2

from competing in the World Championships the following year, even though I had been selected to shoot, but 1982 saw a return to the regular team. A fairly acceptable performance at the European Championships in Hungary took me to tenth place overall and to one of my most satisfying distance awards – Bronze at 30m, which at the time I considered to be my weakest distance. In the autumn I shot in the Commonwealth Games in Brisbane, Australia. It was a memorable trip, and the Games certainly lived up to their reputation for friendliness. Although the opposition were not as formidable as one would find at a World Championship, the tournament was well organised and I had one of my finest moments in winning the Gold Medal.

Owing to developments in my professional career, I did not obtain selection for the 1983 World Championships or the 1984 Olympic Games. This saddened me because I would have liked to compete in both. However, in 1985 I was selected to shoot in the World Championships

Fig 3

Fig 4

held in Korea, where I came a disappointing 44th. The highlight of the trip was Pauline Edwards' magnificent fourth place in the ladies' event. The 1986 trip to Turkey for the European Championships was quite pleasing for me. Despite a dreadful 70m, I came 14th. During the year as a whole, however, I felt that my shooting was better than

ever. Fairly consistent middle 1200 average scores in the FITA Stars bore this out.

I would love to continue my involvement with international archery, but my career demands ever increasing attention. I cannot continue making the same sacrifices as in the past, which is particularly galling because I believe I am shooting bet-

ter than ever and have learned the right way to approach an important tournament in order to achieve a good performance. But I know I am not the first person to want an old head on young shoulders, and realise, too, that because I am an amateur it will be increasingly difficult for me to compete against athletes who are virtually professionals.

TECHNIQUE

Basic Philosophy

My basic approach has always been to keep it simple, the theory being that if something is simple then it is more easily repeated under pressure. It must also feel comfortable and natural. I believe that one or two principles must be adhered to regardless of whatever else you do. Apart from these, an individual's technique will be dictated by physical attributes such as length of forearm, length of neck, shape of chin and so on.

When I am at full draw and on aim, I do not concentrate on pulling the bow. Instead, I concentrate on feeling what I want to achieve after the shot has gone and on how effortless it is to draw the bow. I have several thought patterns that help me to complete the shot, including concentrating on the pressure at either end (on the bow hand and rear elbow). The shot then takes me by surprise, because the click and the actual shooting of the arrow are not a prime consideration at the time when the shot is at its most critical point. That point is certainly not the time to decide whether to shoot. If such a conscious decision ever enters the mind while the arrow is still in the bow, the shot must be let down immediately. The decision whether to shoot must be made before you come up to full draw. The first moment's hesitation should trigger a let-down reaction.

Follow-through is much talked about. I have always believed that it

Fig 5 Foot position.

happens automatically when you think about the correct things just prior to the shot being released. The feeling desired at the end of the shot, and your concentration upon that feeling, is not the same thing as saying to yourself 'Oh, I must remember to follow through' after the shot is released. The most critical moments are just prior to the shot being released and during the fraction of a second after the string has left the fingers. I have always attempted to divorce these from any conscious decision-making. Otherwise, at a time when things happen very quickly you are attempting to make an evaluation of the shot as well as maintaining tension and control.

As a result, you usually forget about the most important factors: the correct thought patterns, the required pressures relative to the target and your concentration on the spot on the target face that you mean to hit.

I like my shots to fall into a rhythm, so I shoot the three arrows of each end in quick succession. This unbroken flow of arrows feels much better than if there had been a deliberate break between each shot. If bad weather forces a break in my rhythm, I play through a number of shots in my mind while I am waiting for a convenient moment to shoot. When I finally do shoot the arrow, it feels like a continuation of the mental sequence.

This method is one of the changes I decided upon during the winter of 1985–86. At the end of every season I look at the way I am shooting and at experiences that arose during the year, then decide what changes I wish to make. I made this particular alteration because I felt my technique was becoming too mechanical, and I wanted more flow and natural feel to the shot. I believe it was a major contribution to a successful year, which was also one of my most enjoyable.

I am wary about making drastic changes, because they generally take a long time to bear fruit. After the Commonwealth Games in 1982, for example, I discarded my anchor tab. Two years of hard practice with a different tab elapsed before I was back to the same standard of shooting. You should be aware of how long it takes to change a system, particularly if you do not have the time necessary to dedicate to it. This is often seen when an archer achieves Master Bowman status then becomes interested in shooting internationally. In the attempt to do even better, he promptly changes a successful technique that he may have been using for years and is surprised to find that his scores and level of expertise fall, even though the new method is potentially superior. Alterations are easier to make when you are experienced, because then you have a better idea of the pressures and results you wish to create.

Belief in your own ability is the key to greater success. I shall remember for a long time being asked at the Grand National Archery Meeting

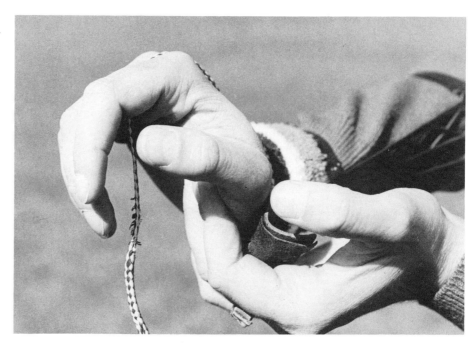

Fig 6a   Pressure point on base of thumb.

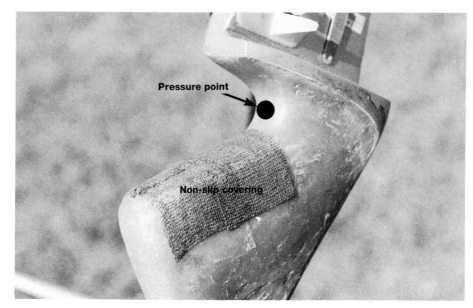

Fig 6b   Pressure point on bow handle grip.

Fig 7a   Predraw tension.

Fig 7b   Predraw tension – back.

Fig 8a   Full draw. Fingers are relaxed around grip.

Fig 8b   Full draw – back view.

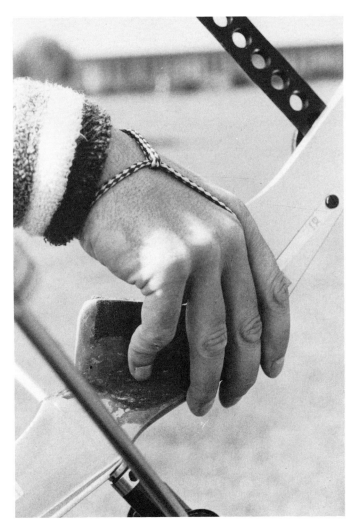

Fig 9a Follow-through. Note the relaxed wrist.

Fig 9b Follow-through – back view.

about the secret to good shooting. At first I thought the person was joking. When I told him about my training schedule and the amount of time I spend shooting, he was no longer smiling. Good shooting, like excellence in any other sport, is based upon many hours of grinding training at times when you would prefer to be doing something else. There is no short route, but I hope that reading about my experiences will help you learn more rapidly.

Making a Shot

As I stand on the shooting line, I feel for the desired alignment relative to the target and move my feet until this is correct. The exact placement of my feet might change from day to day. A good base is important. I concentrate on the pressure on my heels and the balls of my feet, and in so doing I relax my legs and feel stable on the ground. I then take a few deep breaths and imagine any tension in my body seeping away on each exhalation. At times of tension I often feel a bit heady and unstable. However, by concentrating on my stomach and bringing the body's centre of balance back to that spot I feel more stable and controlled than when the centre feels as though it is in the lungs or chest. I stand tall by pushing the crown of my head upwards, which gives a feeling of power. I then look at the target and feel a shot going into the middle of the gold.

When I am mentally ready to shoot the arrow, I locate my hand on the bow by feel. This is most impor-

Fig 10a   Predraw.

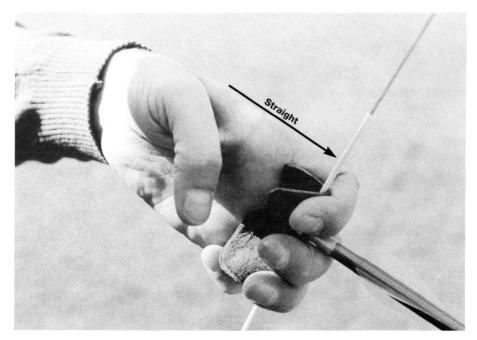

Fig 10b   Predraw.

tant because contact with the bow is the last indirect contact with the arrow. I have always ensured that my hand is comfortable, even if it means building my own handle. I try to feel the pressure on the end of the forearm so that the hand itself is bypassed. This reduces variations caused by differing pressure points in the hand.

Next I place my fingers on the string and take the pressure just behind the first joints, relaxing the back of my hand and ensuring that it is straight and not twisted over at the top. I then concentrate on the target once again and draw slightly until I feel a heavy pressure between the front arm and rear elbow. I come to a three-quarter draw position, then ease back to full draw without stopping. At this stage I once again use visualisation. I have a number of systems, one being to imagine a tube between me and the target. I place both arms into the tube and just imagine easing along that line. I feel secure that the shot will be successful; my arms cannot deviate from the intended plane because they would be stopped by the tube walls. I use various mental pictures according to what seems right at the time. Finally I concentrate on feeling the heavy pressure on both extremities, and the shot will automatically release at some stage.

Fig 11   Fingers coming under load.

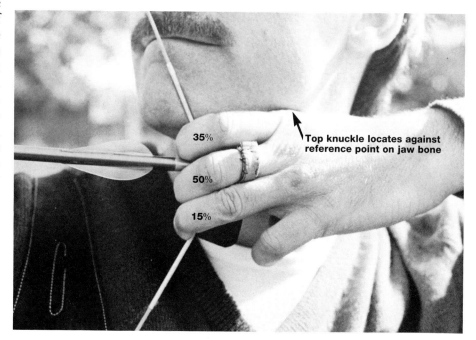

Fig 12   Balance of pressures at full draw.

Fig 13   Full draw. Note the relaxed thumb lying close
        to the neck. The little finger is also relaxed.

Fig 14   Follow-through.

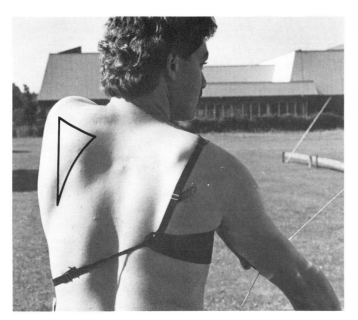

Fig 15   Predraw. Note: there is no conscious *control
of any set of muscles throughout the shot
sequence.*

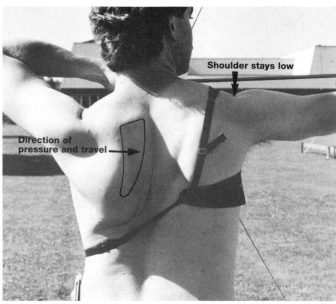

Fig 16   Full draw.

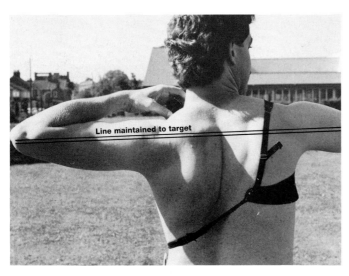

Fig 17   Follow-through with pressures maintained.

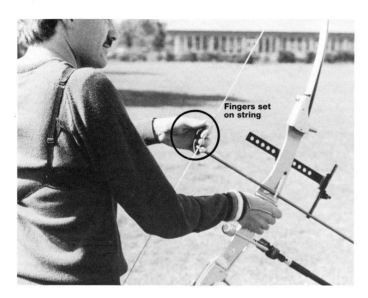

Fig 18   Preparation.

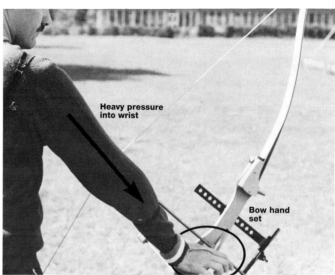

Fig 19   Predraw.

Fig 20   Full draw. Direction of pressure felt from shoulder-blade to wrist.

Fig 21   Follow-through. Pressure maintained and bow arm position held.

PRESSURE CONTROL

Fig 22 illustrates the average archer's draw pressure in relation to the shot's timing. Many have a good, powerful pull until they are at full draw, but it dwindles as the arrow point is pulled through the clicker and the shot is released. When I talk about pulling the bow, it is perhaps more accurately described as expanding the line of force that is felt between handle and string. This gives a picture of the archer overcoming and controlling the growing pressure of the entire shot process (Fig 23), rather than fighting to hold

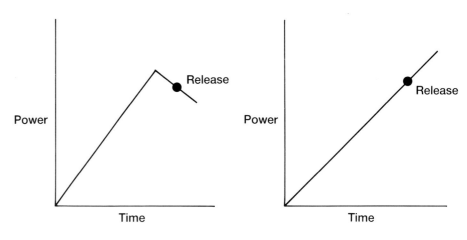

Fig 22   Incorrect pressure control.

Fig 23   Correct pressure control.

Fig 24   Beginning of draw.

Fig 25a   Almost at full draw.

Fig 25b   Almost at full draw.

Fig 26   Full draw pressure points.

Fig 27a   Follow-through.

Fig 27b   Follow-through.

the string back at a fixed full draw position with tensed muscles. Too many archers use too much effort in drawing. By imagining that the arrow is slightly longer than it really is, I maintain pressure between the two ends until the shot releases itself.

I always ensure that my front shoulder is seated low and forward so that there is less chance of it lifting, particularly when I am tired. A lifting shoulder is a major failing because the whole shot feels different and the front end is weak, which is fatal to good scores. Associated with this is the importance of using the correct back muscles, particularly on the rear shoulder. The rear arm should be as passive as possible with the back shoulder unit moving to draw the bow (this can be seen in Figs 24 to 27a). The degree to which the rear shoulder is in line and the level of control on the end of the rear elbow give some indication of how much pressure is on the archer's back. They are only an approximate assessment, however. Physical attributes determine if any individual archer can shoot in line; his level of control is a more important factor.

Fig 28   Predraw.

Fig 29a   Full draw with pressure line established.

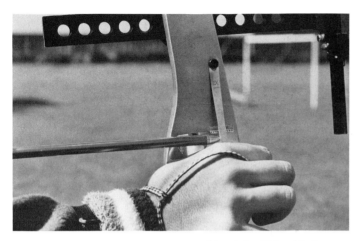

Fig 29b Full draw. Point is within ⅛in of the clicker blade.

Fig 30 Immediately after release. Pressure and line are maintained.

Fig 31 Follow-through.

CLICKER CONTROL

Overall, the important factor is control. The arrow should come to within $\frac{1}{8}$–$\frac{3}{16}$in of clicking on the initial draw, then ease through. However, the draw should never actually stop between these two stages. When a top class shooter is on aim just prior to the shot, it appears as if there is no obvious drawing movement in his arms even though the arrow continues to move relative to the clicker. Concentrate on *feeling* the increasing *pressure*, not on physically moving the arrow.

RELEASE PHASE

At the moment of release my concentration is focused firstly on the pressures along the imaginary tube directed at the target and secondly on what I will feel like at the moment of follow-through. The release itself then becomes automatic. I am not consciously aware that my fingers relax when the clicker goes off.

Fig 32   Release: 1.

Fig 33   Release: 2.

Fig 34   Release: 3.

Fig 35   Release: 4.

TRAINING

After you have forged a sound basic technique, physical and mental training become the most important factors in achieving high performance levels. I approach training on the basis that better scores worldwide will come from an increase in fitness. Many of the world's top shooters are obviously fitter than their counterparts of ten years ago. While at college I was keen to undertake fitness training and found a small gymnasium in Coventry. During that period I was fitter than I had ever been, or have been since. This showed in my performances during 1979 and 1980.

I am fortunate in that I enjoy running. It is a time when I do a lot of thinking without any interruptions. In summer I run three miles three to four times a week. I prefer to run in the early morning when there are few people around and the air is fresh. Running on grass is more enjoyable and also better for the knees and joints than hard concrete pavements. Modern running shoes do have cushioned soles to prevent damage caused by road running, though. It is a sign of the times that everyone expects to see runners on the streets; I can recall being viewed with suspicion by pedestrians during my training runs.

Running develops a good aerobic system and a rich supply of oxygen to the brain and muscles – important benefits when you are faced with an exhausting four-day tournament with its gradual mental and physical drain. I want to be able to shoot the last dozen arrows of the fourth day with as much ease and control as the first dozen on the first day.

The other side of my physical training has developed over a period. With the assistance of a number of people, notably Eddie Robinson while I was a member of the Olympic Training Squad, I approach training on the basis that it will assist me in shooting better. It is not an end in itself, for bulky muscles are not required in archery and can be a hindrance. I use small weights with many repetitions. One winter I worked very hard on fitness and did little shooting. At the beginning of the outdoor season in March, I could pull the bow extremely easily but could not sense the 'feel' of the shot process or the line of pressure directed towards the target. Without these vital sensations I could not feel whether I would hit the left or right of the red. Consequently I ceased weight training and concentrated instead on shooting and trying to produce the right feedback and a precise feeling of direction.

As far as shooting practice is concerned, I like to shoot a lot of arrows in a short time then pack up and do something else. Generally I do not shoot for hours on end, as I used to when doing my groundwork. On vacation from college, I used to shoot all day, every day. I do not require the same number of arrows now that I know the feelings and results I wish to obtain. I do not depend on the number of arrows shot, nor repetition, to achieve good results, especially at major tournaments. However, there are many times when I just enjoy shooting for its own sake and have little direction to what I am doing, even though this is supposed to be contrary to the accepted method of achieving higher standards. The bottom line, though, is that I shoot because I enjoy it; to be a member of the national team is a bonus. I still enjoy the physical act of drawing a bow and releasing arrows. The day I do not, I expect I shall stop altogether.

When there is a particular item to practise, I identify it beforehand and therefore give a clear aim to the session. At various times I go systematically through my whole technique to check that everything is working as it should. Because archery is basically the same action whatever the distance, I find that I become lazy and lapse into bad habits. This is why I check the system. Also, the more closely you look at yourself, the better your understanding becomes. Problems are thus more easily solved when they do occur. When I start to shoot poorly, I find it comforting to know that the action I am reproducing is correct and that it looks as though it performs well. This being so, it is not long before my scores are back to their normal level.

Fig 36

Fig 37

Fig 38

Fig 39

Fig 40

Fig 41

Fig 42

Fig 43

Fig 44

Fig 45

Fig 46

THINKING AND FEELING

For a long time I have been fascinated by how the mind can affect performance. I am a great believer in visualisation and use it when shooting and at other times. I often find myself thinking my way through a shot when I am walking along the road, during a pause at work or when sitting in a chair. Visualisation is important because the feelings and thought processes are the same as if you were actually shooting. To begin with, it is better to do the exercises at home in a quiet environment where you will not be disturbed.

I start by relaxing and closing my eyes. I feel myself and see myself walking up to the line and standing astride it. Then I go through the same steps as if I were shooting an arrow; I feel the shot *and* its follow-through. Once this has been perfected until it becomes second nature, you will find it possible mentally to shoot a few arrows with no need to lie down, close your eyes and relax. I often do this during the day to refresh myself from work, and because it is a form of practice. (Don't tell the boss that you practise archery at work!) One advantage is that you greatly increase the number of arrows shot. It has been shown that neurological grooves are set just as much by visualisation as by actually shooting. It is an invaluable method during adverse weather or when injury prevents you from shooting. As I have progressed in technical skill, I find that I need to shoot less and less provided that I exercise sufficiently

to control the bow properly and keep up my visualisation programme.

Visualisation helps just prior to a tournament and when you are shooting. If I 'feel' a few mental shots before actually starting, I am less tense and also have a clearer mind about what I want to achieve that day. On the line, I quickly visualise a shot just prior to shooting an end. Tensions are reduced because making each shot is merely a question of reproducing an already-visualised action.

A few days before a tournament, be it national, international or merely a local shoot, I always spend a few moments sitting quietly and imagining (visualising) what the scene will be. At larger shoots in Great Britain I will know the ground in question and can be more accurate in my visualisation. I see myself arriving, establishing myself on the line and shooting. It does not matter if your target number turns out to be different from what you imagined; the important point is that you have experienced the ground and will consequently feel more at ease there. Visualisation is more effective if all sensory perceptions are used: smell, taste, touch and hearing, as well as sight. Some grounds have certain anomalies, and they should be included in your mental picture.

Before travelling abroad I place myself on the field and visualise all the pomp and ceremony associated with international shoots. Unless you are careful, they can be a distraction. I try to see just the target and the shooting line with me astride it. This picture will be exactly the same

regardless of whether I am on the practice field or the Olympic tournament ground. The picture will not be strictly accurate until I have arrived at the venue itself. Then, in the evenings during the run-up to the start of shooting, I spend a few moments relaxing on my bed and gradually drift into feeling myself shoot on that particular ground. When the tournament begins, the field does not seem so alien.

It is generally accepted that repeating any experience makes you less apprehensive about each subsequent performance. Nerves subside, and your enjoyment of the occasion takes over. I have used the method to great effect in other areas of life, such as interviews and important events at work.

Many sportsmen consider that staying on top is more difficult than getting there in the first place. I agree. It has always surprised me how many archers achieve good results one year but find it difficult to produce the same performance the next season. Perhaps the variation is due to their own or other people's expectations, or a combination of both. The important thing is to enjoy shooting and hitting the middle rather than making some particular score or tournament success the prime objective. Concentrate on the action and feeling of each shot rather than the end result of each arrow and the tournament.

A thread running through my approach is to try and take any important decision away from the time when it has its most critical effect. For instance, I believe that the wrong time to decide to shoot is after the clicker has clicked. Consequently, the decision to shoot should be made at the approach stage instead. When any hesitation enters the mind, the shot has probably been lost and should therefore be let down and set up again.

The act of winning also needs to be visualised. I react well to tournaments and enjoy the intense competition of climbing the leader board. I am spurred towards higher performance this way. I also like to watch other sports and see individuals or teams in a winning situation. Again, it helps improve my own performance. When training, I often imagine shooting in a world event where I need a particular score and have only a few arrows left. The mental effect is similar to visualisation; it makes you familiar with the feeling of shooting under pressure. When it actually happens, the real situation feels less alien. I also enjoy shooting on a noisy field or with a radio playing close by. Distractions are many and various. If you are to be successful, they must not interfere with your performance or thought processes. I find that as a result of visualisation and mental practice, the greater the distraction, the more intense my concentration becomes.

Ultimately, you should be able to divorce yourself entirely from outside interference. At the European Championships in 1978 I had what is commonly called an out-of-body experience, as though I were detached from my body and floating. I felt very little tension and shot close to my best performance at that time.

Fig 47

Fig 48

Fig 49

Fig 50

The experience prompted my interest in the mental approach. Nobody within the sport could help me, so I looked outside. In 1979 I attended an 'Inner Tennis' course and was astounded that by the end of the day I was capable of having long rallies of up to twenty strikes down between the tramlines – dramatic results considering that previously I had played next to no tennis.

Through my brother, who is a professional golfer and whose friend, Sandy Dunlop, started it, I was introduced to the 'Sporting Bodymind', a development programme which relates sporting performance to mental approach. I worked intensively with Christopher Connelly, one of the leaders, over the next few months and became aware of body movements that I had not concentrated upon before. This gave me greater understanding of my own technique and led to methods of reducing the feelings of tension under stress, especially at important tournaments. The system enables me to approach a tournament more positively and with confidence, knowing that I can perform at the level at which I think I am capable.

Fig 51

Fig 52

Fig 53

Fig 54

EQUIPMENT

My feelings on equipment follow those on technique: keep it simple. I tend to select equipment on the basis that if it is simple to set up, it will not let me down at a vital time. This is an important factor in shooting at international tournaments. It is tempting to try a stabilisation set-up or new piece of equipment because somebody else is shooting with it, for example. Everyone, including the top shooters, suffer from this fallacy, but I always evaluate an unfamiliar system or item beforehand. Ultimately, whether I use it depends on its feel as much as on the results. I believe that satisfaction with the feel increases scores anyway.

In recent years I have concentrated on achieving good limb operation as the basis of tuning. Limbs must recover together, otherwise a rocking motion can be seen when the bow is viewed from some distance to one side. Before I started to shoot Greenhorn bows, I would alter the limbs by sanding off the face where it attached to the handle. The advent of the adjustable tiller makes life much easier.

I begin tuning the limb reaction on a bare bow by flicking the string close to one end and seeing how long the rocking motion takes to subside. Then I add the required stabiliser system and go through the rough tuning procedure again. When the best reaction is achieved I start shooting, preferably at long range. I feel the bow's reaction and fine-tune it until it becomes smooth.

At this stage I am not unduly con-

Fig 55   Keep it simple!

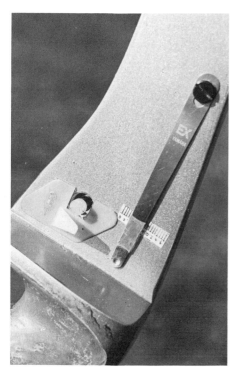

Fig 56 Arrow rest and clicker set-up.

Fig 57 Plain aperture sight with 4mm ring (2mm internal diameter).

cerned about arrow flight, although I have, of course, set up the equipment beforehand so that arrows leave the bow reasonably well. As a starting point, the arrow is placed outside centre-shot. I believe it is a mistake to set the button on centre because paradox comes into effect when the departing arrow depresses the plunger. The shaft therefore moves inside of centre-shot, which is an unstable and critical position. One point to watch when lining up the arrow is that both limbs are unimpeded and that the centre of the *limbs* is used as

the reference point. Do not align the string with the fixing system of the bow because these components can be slightly off-centre.

Having achieved the best feeling, I can start to fine-tune and concentrate on arrow flight. In 1978 I was lucky enough to be coached by John Williams, the 1971 World Champion and 1972 Olympic Champion. Since

then much of my thinking has been influenced by what I learned from him, in particular the method I use to set up my bow. I have never deviated from it because I have been unable to discover a system that produces better arrow flight.

Initially I set the nocking point $\frac{1}{8}$in above the right angle to the bottom of my nock. I have always found that I shoot with a high nocking point even when the limbs are properly tuned, because of my personal pressure point on the handle. A slightly high point is better than one that is too low, because with the latter the fletchings hit the arrow rest. Next I shoot a bare shaft at two to three yards, ensuring that I hold the bow so that the arrow is drawn parallel to the ground. Otherwise, the impact angle of the arrow in the target would give a false reading even though the nocking point is correct.

I then use the conventional walk-back test, shooting fletched arrows from ten to forty yards. Finally, I run a bare shaft versus fletched shaft comparison test at 12 yards. Using a number of read-outs gives me confidence that the equipment is functioning properly. I carefully record all the settings so that the bow can be set up the same way again at any time. Finally, I like to check how the arrows fly at long range. It is difficult to see them for myself, so I ask somebody to observe while I shoot at 70 or 90 metres.

Steve Hallard

MY ARCHERY CAREER

I started shooting in 1976 when I was ten years old. As a junior I entered many tournaments, thus gaining a tremendous wealth of knowledge even by the age of fifteen. With strong parental support I was encouraged to enter senior tournaments, but was always allowed to do what I wanted and never pressurised. Too many parents pressurise their children, which kills their interest in the end. I was lucky.

In 1980 I met Barry Farndon and his wife June, who are now my personal coaches and friends. Barry showed me my own potential to be an international archer, and perhaps a world champion some day. We met at a local FITA Star and within three weeks I put 300 points on my single FITA score to break the British junior record of 1228. I think I was the youngest holder of a 1200 FITA Star at the time. Since then I have grown from strength to strength under Barry's careful guidance. One question that he likes to use to test people's motivation and attitude is: would you cycle 40 miles to go shooting? The answers are usually negative; but I did exactly that. This is one example of how strong my will is – and how strong *your* attitude must be if you want to get to the top.

In 1981 I broke the British FITA record for the first time with 1265 (I was sixteen at the time) and in the following year I pushed it to 1299. Although I have only once bettered that score to collect my Red 1300 FITA Star, I am firmly convinced that I am on the road to success. Despite what the critics said, I am still here and still winning. Goals for the future are quite simple: a medal in the World, European or Olympic Championships would satisfy my hunger – for a little while!

PUTTING A GOOD SHOT TOGETHER

Stance

The stance that I have adopted is generally referred to as 'open', which gives me increased upper body stability with the feet comfortably apart and the rest of the body totally relaxed. Note that a line drawn across my toes points considerably away from the target. It is most important to keep relaxed and not to force anything. I just stand how I feel comfortable. In bad weather I increase the gap between my feet and open the stance to the target; this increases my upper body torque and hence gives extra stability when I am on aim and running the shot process.

Fig 58

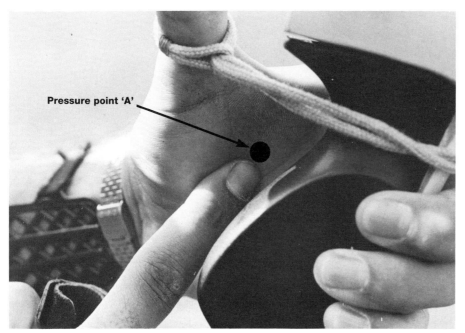

Pressure point 'A'

Fig 59a

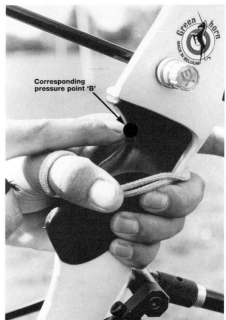

Corresponding pressure point 'B'

Fig 59b

The Bow Arm Unit

Generally I have adopted a low wrist action on the bow handle because it gives me a more consistent reaction when the shot process takes place. Point 'A' indicates where I pin-point the main pressure force, and 'B' shows the corresponding position on the bow grip.

The hand is at the preloaded stage with the string lightly tensed so that I can position it exactly where I want. I must stress that it is very important to keep everything relaxed. Under no circumstances do I attempt to force anything.

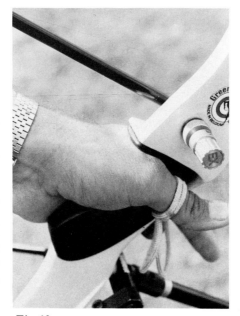

Fig 60a

Fig 60b

String Hand and Follow-through

My finger arrangements on the string: probably the part of my technique on which I have worked the most. For years I developed the two finger release – that is, only holding weight on the fingers nearest to the arrow. I have recently had to adopt the present pattern because of finger damage (Fig 63).

My hand is relaxed with the predraw pressure on it (Fig 64).

Fig 61

Fig 62

Relaxed bow hand with the knuckles at an approximate angle of 45 degrees to the bow.

The natural reaction of the bow hand unit on release.

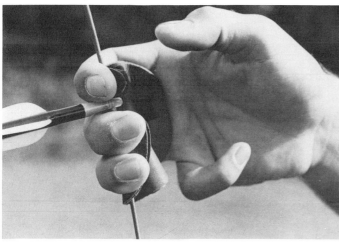

Fig 63

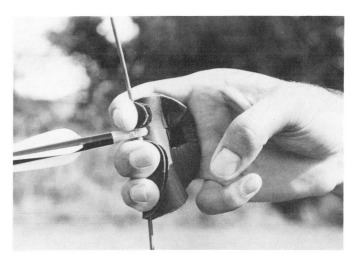

Fig 64

Fig 65a

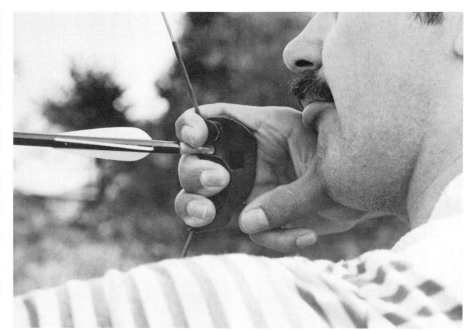

Fig 65b

As the sequence of the shot continues, the fingers have equal pressure on them and the drawing hand is kept close to my face. This makes sure that the shot is kept in line and that the power increase keeps moving in a straight line.

The all-important anchor. I am a firm believer in having a positive anchor with as many reference points as possible.

Fig 66

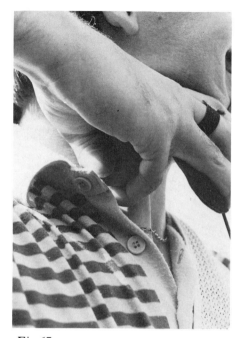 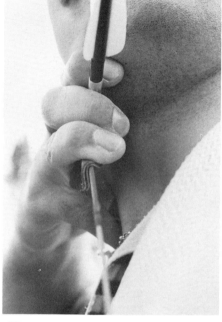

The thumb is behind my neck, the little finger behind the guide and the top of my hand running firmly along the jaw bone. The anchor is achieved by the roll-over wrist technique and hence it is important to rotate from the wrist and not actually move the fingers. Note that the back of my hand is flat and relaxed and the fingers are not pulling any weight.

Fig 67a   *Fig 67b*

 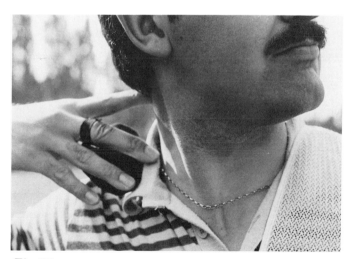

Fig 68a   *Fig 68b*

The release with the hand rolling over, keeping contact with my neck.

The top two fingers finish behind my neck.

Fig 69a

Fig 69b

TYPICAL SHOT SEQUENCE

The shot itself begins to build up from the moment I step across the shooting line. My feet automatically position themselves at the angle which I feel is required. I do not like using foot markers because although you set them up at the beginning of the day's shooting the conditions of both your body and the tournament can prompt changes in stance as the day progresses.

Predraw position. At this point the shot is mentally put together. The fingers are positioned on the string relative to the arrow, and with a little more tension the bow hand is settled into place.

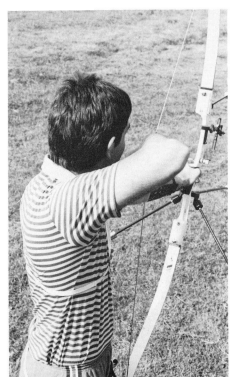

Fig 70b

Fig 70a

Throughout the drawing process both arms are gradually loaded until the anchor is achieved. (The drawing process does not stop there though; pressure is applied until the shot is made.)

Fig 71a

Fig 71b

Fig 72a

Fig 72b

Once the anchor is achieved, the draw length is checked visually and the sight aligned with the target.

Fig 73a

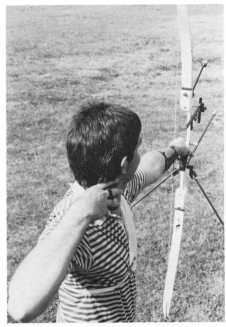

Fig 73b

Finally, after the draw checks are complete the explosion happens. Note that the arrow is almost clear of the bow, but the drawing position is virtually unaltered.

Fig 74a

Fig 74b

The follow-through completes itself, with the back hand keeping close to the neck and the bow hand staying up with the shot so that I do not disrupt the arrow's path out of the bow. My eyes remain on the point at which I aimed to ensure that I do not peek around the bow; in other words, do not move the bow out of the way to see where the shot went. If I do peek, I usually affect the path of the arrow or begin to anticipate the release, consequently moving my bow before the arrow hits the target.

BACK TENSION

Back tension is probably the most important aspect of archery. In good back tension I have found the secret of high scores and winning. Watch the action of the elbow as the shot sequence progresses. I must stress here that I concentrate on the elbow's *position* and on the *feel* that develops as a result. To help explain how back tension develops I have indicated which muscle zones are used, but I do *not* think about them while the shot process is running.

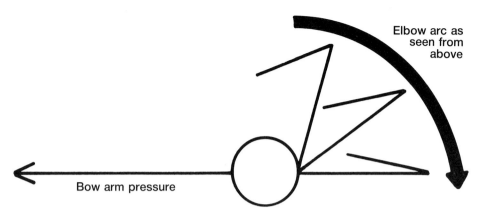

Fig 75   Elbow control.

Personally, I find that keeping the elbow elevated and high as the draw takes place helps to create good back tension.

Fig 76a

Fig 76b

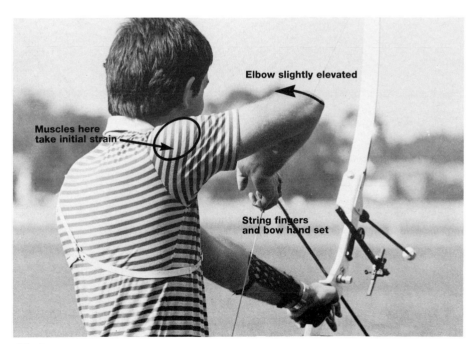

Fig 76c

Although the elbow has now dropped from the initially high draw position, back tension has developed.

Fig 77a

The result – a smooth release that flows behind the neck.

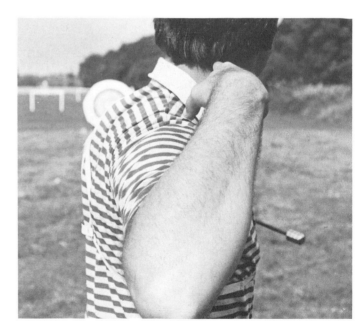

Fig 78a

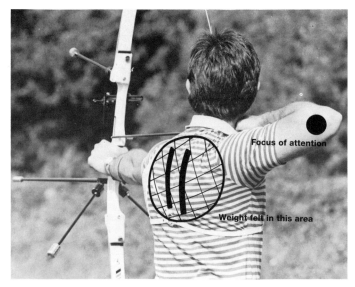

Fig 77b

Fig 77c

Fig 78b

Fig 78c

PRESSURES, CLICKER CONTROL AND CONCENTRATION

Fig 79

Bow hand and drawing fingers are set, and my eyes concentrate on the gold.

Fig 80

During the predraw, I watch the arrow and clicker. I feel the draw pressures beginning to build up at the front and back.

Fig 81

The draw pressures continue to build, and the elbow moves through the correct arc. My eyes flick back and forth between the gold and the clicker to control the length.

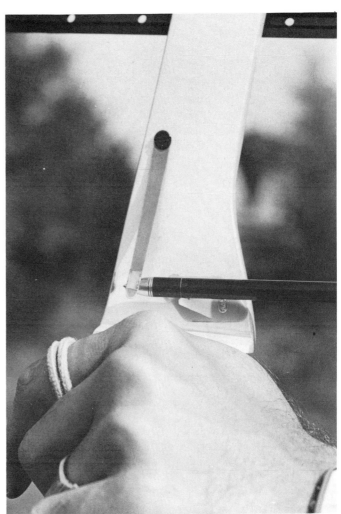

Fig 82

Good length control. I have anchored and achieved the desired 'feel'.

Fig 83

Fig 84

Now I concentrate all my attention on aiming. The two ends expand, and my fingers relax when the clicker goes off. Owing to good back tension, my forefinger stays in contact with my jawbone.

Follow-through. I 'stay with the shot' until the arrow hits the target. My eyes remain focused on the gold, and my stance is upright and solid. Draw fingers are relaxed, with the knuckles at about 45 degrees to vertical.

AIMING AND STRING ALIGNMENT

One thing is certain: you can never shoot as accurately as you are capable of aiming. The technique that I have adopted for several years now is to bounce the pin on the bottom of the gold, thus keeping the upper body relaxed and not trying to over-aim. At the shorter distances when over-aiming is more likely to occur I usually let the pin wander around the 10 ring. Instead of trying to *hit* the 10 ring, I try *not to miss* it.

So far as string alignment goes, I have always used a method of picture aiming. This is quite a simple process where you teach yourself to get used to seeing the picture that develops at full draw. As long as the picture looks familiar, you continue to shoot without thinking consciously about lining up the string with the relevant point on the bow. If for any reason something alters, though, you will instantly recognise it. Then you can identify the cause.

Fig 85

Fig 86

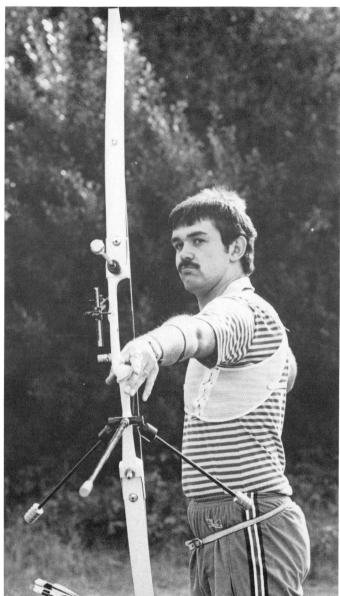

Fig 87

THINKING AND FEELING

When in practice or at a tournament, I must remember that I am trying to achieve one correct shot. Over the years my shot has evolved to its present look and feel. It is no good just coming up and shooting an arrow; anyone can do that. The correct way is to prepare the shot properly so that I can feel the process throughout its different stages. I teach myself how to feel the shot both mentally and physically. It is difficult to explain, but actually quite simple.

When the shot happens it is effortless, and I do not really know where it came from. I cannot explain what happened; but I do know how it felt and I also know how to reproduce it. A good method of building the feel is to shoot at a blank boss with your eyes shut. By not consciously aiming, I find that I can analyse the shot right through and get to know exactly how it feels. Once I know how the process is built up physically and what it feels like, I begin working on my mental approach.

There are two main aspects to archery. Basic archery is concerned with form, but championship archery is a purely mental game. What I think about when I shoot is very important to me. I want no negative thoughts creeping into the pattern of the shooting process, and consequently have to put something in my mind to keep them out. Over the past two or three years I have concentrated very hard on aiming, thus divorcing my mind from the shot process. I have already trained

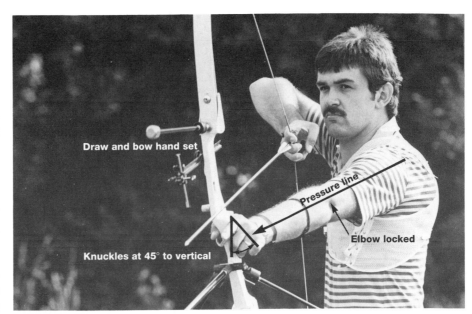

Fig 88   Predraw.

Fig 89   Coming towards anchor.

and conditioned myself physically by shooting at close range, so I know exactly how the shot feels. Therefore if my mind allows my body to shoot that well-trained sequence, I can execute almost perfect form. If so, I have achieved the ultimate goal of being in total control of myself and any situation that could confront me. I go to a tournament to shoot; I am not there looking for errors in my form. I have always believed that if you do not take it with you, you will not find it at the tournament.

From the first arrow of the tournament I am shooting for feel. If a bad arrow occurs – and everyone has them, let me tell you – I try not to think about it or dwell upon it. Those are negative responses. The same applies if I take it out on my equipment. I have seen binoculars and bows thrown and stabilisers broken, but what does this achieve? It proves that you are not in control of yourself and that you will never attain the ultimate goal of high scores. I overcome this by accepting things as they are, and carry on trying to put the feel together again. Some days I find that no matter what I do, the arrows go in the middle. I also have days when I cannot hit the middle whatever I do. It happens to everybody. But if you have a good solid foundation to your shooting, as I do, the black days do not last very long and become fewer and further apart.

Total concentration is probably the most difficult thing to achieve. When you consider that the shot happens in about one-hundredth of a second, concentration must be one

Fig 90 Anchor.

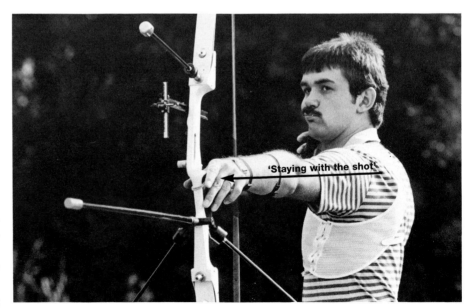

Fig 91 Explosion.

Fig 92   Follow-through.

hundred per cent otherwise you are not going to achieve a constant feel or a controlled atmosphere. If concentration level is high, all I do is feel for the shot process. If it falls, adverse aspects are allowed to creep in and destroy the control of the shot, groups open up and scores go down.

I find that it helps to look at the gold throughout the shot. If my concentration level is high enough, I seem to will the arrow into the centre. Consequently I try to shoot in my subconscious mind and thus work with myself to help myself. Apart from the feel of the shot and the highly directed sense of concentration, I think and feel nothing else. Obviously my eyes and ears are monitoring everything that is going on around me. If anything happens, such as the wind increases in strength, I automatically adjust for it. I never consider what I am doing; my subconscious shoots the arrows for me. This is the secret of winning and will give you the score levels you wish, even if you lack the ideal physical form. Remember though: never think about winning. If you do, you are on a losing streak. Concentrate purely on shooting that one correct shot and that one shot alone.

EQUIPMENT AND TUNING

Over the past eleven years I have arrived at what I look for in equipment by logically analysing it for any definite advantages or disadvantages. If the advantages outweigh the disadvantages, I usually end up using it. I do not fall into the trap of being distracted by glossy pictures and clever advertising. Archery is a gimmick-ridden sport, so beware.

What I look for in a bow is good solid design in both handle and limbs. The handle must be straight; that is, when the bow is strung and you line up the string with the middle of the top of the riser, it also cuts through the corresponding point on the bottom of the riser. The limbs must be stable and react together in a balanced manner, which can usually only be seen by somebody watching you shooting the bow. You do not want the limbs flapping about after the arrow has cleared the bow. If they do, they probably do it while the arrow is leaving as well.

I have always made my own strings. You can trust those you make more than you can shop-bought ones. Quality and length can be controlled exactly. When somebody else makes a string, you never know what they have done to it. There could be some hidden horror under the serving.

I choose arrows in a similar way to that in which I pick a bow: by looking for shafts and fletching arrangements that give me the best results. Arrows are generally selected from the maker's chart by picking a suit-

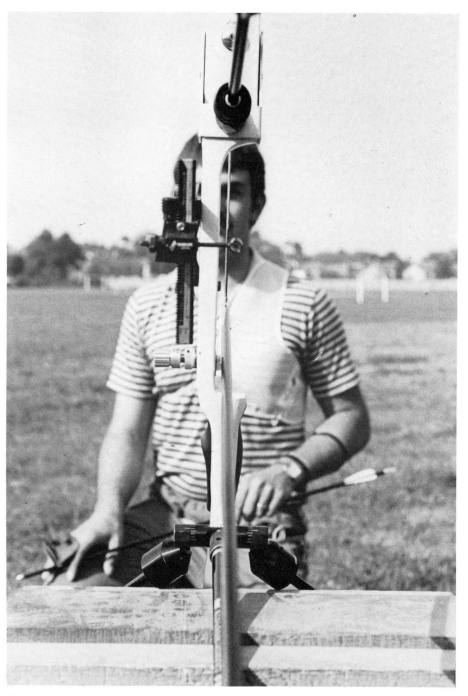

Fig 93 Centre-shot adjustment.

able balance of spine against weight. I use 2115 shafts because at my draw length and weight they are the only specification I can use. People shooting less weight and length are at an advantage because they can choose from several shaft specifications. I have found that a vane with helical fletching flies with greater stability than one with straight fletching. Probably the most important point to make about arrows is that the nock must be attached correctly. Unless it is straight you will never achieve consistent grouping. If the swaging becomes damaged, I scrap the arrow because I do not wish to run the risk of shooting an unbalanced shaft.

Tuning

Bow tuning is done simply. First the bow is set up on centre-shot: note where the string cuts through the sight pin. This allows adjustment of windage both ways and reassures me that I could not lose the pin behind the bow in a strong left to right wind. The pressure button is wound out until the arrow has just passed bow centre, and the spring pressure is set to medium. At approximately 10–12 yards and aiming at a target pin, I shoot a pattern of three fletched and one unfletched shafts.

Tuning is correct when the fletched and unfletched shafts group together. However, this is only a coarse tuning programme. What counts is how the arrows fly. On the whole, a pressure button only positions the sight; it does not make much difference to the arrow's flight pattern. I usually ask a friend to see

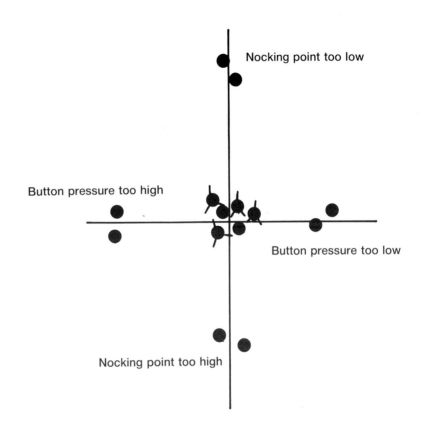

Fig 94   Impact pattern.

how the arrows are performing in the air, because I have found that although tests on a blank boss are all right, it might still be essential to alter fletching angles and arrangements to produce optimum flight and grouping.

TOURNAMENT TACTICS

Preparation is probably the key to success when you get to the tournament itself. Small details can and do make all the difference between winning and losing. Where is the tournament; how will I get there or where will I stay; what is the round and what time will it start? Once I know all this, I can schedule myself accordingly. I also ask myself whether the bow is set up and arrows and strings are in good shape. Am I happy with my own form and general conditions?

Everything must be right, otherwise I arrive with doubts as to whether I can compete for four days on end without problems. I also take the unexpected into account – for example, I always go prepared for any weather even though the forecast is hot and sunny. Never trust anyone except yourself, because others can let you down. My mind must also be in gear; any personal problems must be cleared up before I get to the tournament otherwise under moments of extreme pressure they might come back into my conscious mind and interfere with the shooting process.

Tournament pressure is an area of archery that is difficult to describe. I have found that pressures which affect most people, including myself, are self-inflicted. I overcome them by building my own world around me, which in itself removes me from the tournament. Consequently, I rise above the event and its pressures. The important point to remember is that the only person you should be

The Perfect Shot

Fig 95

shooting against is yourself – not Joe Bloggs ten targets further down the line.

As I have already said, you must be prepared for adverse conditions. Wind can destroy an archer physically and mentally, for example. I overcome the problems of wind by re-

membering that wherever a gust comes from or goes to, it will also affect the other archers on the line. Wind always seems to drop when the other detail is shooting, but it always evens out by the end of the day to affect everyone equally. I prefer to let the wind take me – in a controlled

Fig 96

Fig 97

fashion, of course – because if I fight it my shooting starts to break down mentally and physically as I begin to weaken. If I allow my body to drift at full draw, when the wind finally does drop I can quickly come on to aim at the allocated position on the target and shoot the arrow down the visual-ly projected curved line into the cen-tre of the target.

Fig 98

Fig 99

Fig 100

Fig 101

MENTAL AND PHYSICAL CONDITIONING

I consider both mental and physical conditioning of myself and my shooting to be very important. Let us look at these in turn: first, the physical side. Conditioning my physical shooting and my body in general comes high on my list of priorities. My physical shooting technique has taken many hours to perfect, as has conditioning myself to shoot totally in my subconscious. It is best for me to have a tailored approach to practising with a time-table of definite objectives and goals at the end of each stage. For example, if I practise the release or follow-through and achieve that goal, then I am happy. If I fail, I have to be honest with myself and ask why – and keep asking until I find the answer.

When I consider the general physical conditioning of my body, I again tailor a programme to definite goals and objectives. My programme has been formulated over many years and is altered on the basis of experience or to suit new requirements. The mainstay is basically to shoot lots of arrows, which to a great extent looks after the physical side. However, throughout the winter I find that additional training is required to stay trim. I do so by exercising the complete body rather than just the parts involved in archery.

My programme consists of stretching and a limited number of weight exercises. Weights are used only to stretch the muscles, not to build them up. Mobility is more

Concentration and Control

Fig 102

Fig 105

Fig 103

Fig 104

Fig 106

Fig 107

important than physical strength; but of course you do need to be strong to shoot a bow all day. I also do a lot of running, 10 to 20 miles a week in the winter, and a few miles a day on an exercise bicycle as well. This is excellent for the heart and lungs and gives me controlled breathing and a lower pulse rate.

The same effort must also be put into mental conditioning. In the past, this has been rather looked down upon, but I find that people are beginning to wake up to the fact that mental conditioning plays a tremendous role in top class archery. Having explored what the powers of the mind can do, I am always surprised how mental conditioning can improve certain aspects, such as handling tournament pressures and nervousness.

I mentally practise shooting arrows at normal speed into the middle of the target. Looking at the middle of a paper face helps the visualisation process by reinforcing the image of arrows hitting the middle of the gold. I also have to be honest with myself; mistakes can so easily be made and it takes a big man to accept some of them. But you and I must accept them because it is the only way to improve. You will never improve by blaming somebody else if the fault actually lies in you.

WHY I AM A BETTER THAN AVERAGE ARCHER

Again, this can be split into two categories. First let's look at the physical side. You could say that I am very fortunate to have been born with two straight arms of the correct proportions and a body that is reasonably fit. With these, I have developed my own personal technique and basic shooting form. Everyone has a different body, so it is up to you to manufacture a shot around what you possess.

Once I had developed a basic technique, I could start building up on my overall control of the shooting. Over the course of years while growing up with archery, my body has developed shooting muscles. My back, shoulder and arm muscles are built differently on the left and right sides of my spinal column, because one side of my body is used in tension (back arm) and the other in compression. From this I have developed technique and power to control the bow totally, making it do what I want.

For the past seven years my technique has been watched closely by my own personal coach, who gives me a breakdown of what is happening and who is an ideal partner to bounce ideas around with. It is very important to have somebody to work with, and also to be surrounded by the right people in a good atmosphere. For example, at the club I shoot at there are many good archers hungry for the same goal. Consequently we learn from each other, which creates a waterfall effect. On this basis I have gone from strength to strength, improving in definite steps. Probably one of the most important factors in my success is to have trained in a good atmosphere. In a bad one, you become involved in things that do not matter.

Attitude is the mainstay of my mental control. With the correct attitude, I have moved and will continue to move mountains. My attitude controls everything I do, including when and what I practise, always working towards the goal of the World Championship. If I single out one aspect of my shooting that puts me in front of the rest, this is it. Attitude also goes hand in hand with the desire to shoot, and ultimately to shoot 10s and thus win tournaments. It takes strong mental control to achieve anything in life, because it is all too easy to walk away or sit in an armchair and dream. Dreams only come true if you work hard at them. We must all work hard and play hard to become the successful people we want to be.

Power and Determination

Fig 108

Fig 109

Fig 110

Fig 111

Fig 112

Fig 113

Best wishes Sylvia
Go for Gold

Philip van Buren

MY ARCHERY CAREER

Apart from boyhood dreams of being Robin Hood, and having street battles with home-made equipment (I now shudder at the thought), my adult interest began at a have-a-go stall when I worked as a designer with British Rail. I joined the Carriage and Wagon Archery Club in 1970 under the guidance of Roy and Beryl Bickerstaffe in Derby. In 1971 I moved back home to Hove and joined the Brighton club, County Oak, where I met my wife (the treasurer's daughter). Over the past sixteen years I have held every committee post, been chairman for seven years and open tournament organiser for thirteen years. In 1979 I was awarded Honorary Life Membership for services to the club.

During my period as Sussex County Coaching Organiser, 1978–86, I founded the Martlets Coaching Guild and became a GNAS Regional Coach in 1982. In 1980 I founded the first ever all-blind archery club in the world at St Dunstan's Home in Brighton. With my assistant Lauri Austin, I developed the tactile sight which is now an integral part of the blind archer's kit. We were the first people to develop the teaching of archery to the blind, and my methods are now practised all over the world. My supreme achievement was to develop shooting aids that allowed a totally blind man, without hands or forearms, to hit the target consistently at 80 yards, thus proving all the pundits wrong.

By 1978 I decided to spend more time shooting, which gave me Master Bowman scores throughout the 1979–1981 period. I was Sussex FITA and field champion in 1979 and a regular county team member from 1978 to 1982. In 1981 I started to shoot the compound in selected field and target events, and have held the Sussex field and indoor titles ever since. In 1982 I won the SCAS Regional Indoor Championships after setting a new British record the previous October at the Sussex Indoors with a 594 Portsmouth.

In 1983 I first entered the Sussex Championships with a compound, winning the title which I have held ever since. I was tied second that year

Power and Control

Fig 114

in the UK Compound Masters Indoor Vegas. In 1984 GNAS allowed compounds to gain Master Bowman status, and I was just pipped to being the first man qualified. So I decided to be first to gain both target and field Master Bowman, which I did in 1985.

I repeated the double in 1986 and now intend to be the first archer to gain Grand Master qualification in both events concurrently. In 1985 I won the UK Masters Championships and the Southern Counties Regional Championships, and in 1986 became national record holder for the York with 1132, FITA Hunter with 489 and National Animal Round with 500. The first two have already been beaten, but I'll have them back – and more!

Fig 115

Fig 116

Fig 117

Fig 118

FUNDAMENTALS

In my opinion, the most essential criteria for consistently good shooting, irrespective of bow design/type or shooting style, are correct and stable posture coupled with a strong but relaxed bow arm and shoulder. I call it a 'flexible prop'. This is the foundation of all my shooting, target or field, and I cannot overstress its importance for continued consistency and for attaining a minimum of Master Bowman standard. Posture became a crucial part of my shooting after I seriously damaged my lower spine in November 1984. Despite a few relapses since, the combination of correct stance and a lumbar support have kept me shooting at the top level, and I hope to go on improving.

I must emphasise that a straight spine – not rigid but relaxed – is the starting point for a good mental build-up to the shot. At the top level, successful archery is mainly about mental control and feel. If I do not stand properly and feel right, I cannot think correctly and consequently do not shoot correctly. 'Feel' is related to many things: intuition, instinct and subjective response, along with more tangible conditions such as physical and mental stress, shooting and weather conditions – in other words the effect of the immediate environment on the archer.

A successful archer will not allow external conditions to affect his inner calm. He remains in control of his emotions and therefore his shooting skills. This is illustrated by the fact that on the day I broke the British record for the York round, I was

Bow Arm and Shoulder Control

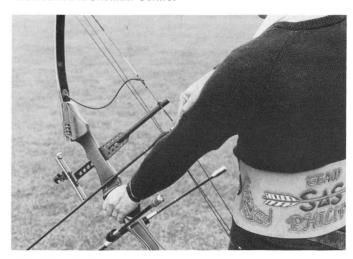

Fig 119   Predraw.

Fig 122   Full draw.

Fig 120 Bow and arm aligned with target.

Fig 121 Bow shoulder settled into position.

Fig 123 Follow-through.

constantly being called to my mobile shop to sell and advise, besides keeping an eye on my family whilst my wife shot alternately with me on the same target (she also shot a York record that day). All these distractions did not deter me from my main purpose of shooting a national record.

SHOOTING SEQUENCE

Before a day's shooting I go through a warm-up routine of exercises to loosen my upper torso, especially my shoulder, back and arm muscles. I also ensure that I keep warm throughout a shoot to prevent me from seizing up; I also loosen up again after the lunch-break. A light warm-down at the end of a shoot expels unwanted lactic acids in the muscles and prevents aches and stiffness.

When approaching the line, I make myself spatially aware of the target and the rest of the environment. I check my body alignment by drawing the bow without an arrow and then holding on aim while I close my eyes for four seconds. The body is allowed to take a natural, uninfluenced line. When I open my eyes, I should still be on the correct aiming point. If not, I adjust my position accordingly and remember my body position relative to the target. This allows me to line up my body with the target each time without using foot markers.

Fig 124

Field archery has contributed greatly to this awareness as well as to my general balance. You will notice that my feet are slightly oblique to the line and just comfortably spaced at approximately hip width.

Fig 125

Resting the long rod on the ground, I secure the wrist sling then relax both mentally and physically before taking the arrow and guiding it on to the string and rest.

Fig 126

Fig 127

Having nocked the arrow, I loop the release rope around the string under the arrow nock using the thumb and index finger.

Fig 128

It is secured on the release peg with my thumb nail to ensure no slippage.

Fig 129

Fig 130

Fig 131

Putting the string under slight tension locks the rope in place and allows the hand to slide to a relaxed but secure position. Now the shot can be set up.

With the back straight and the head raised, I set my bow hand to its relaxed position with the pressure on the ball of the palm.

The bow shoulder is consciously lowered until the scapula is felt next to the spine. The feel is good and relaxed. Keeping the shoulder down and the head up, I breath in deeply as I raise the bow until the grip is at approximately eye level and the drawing elbow is horizontally opposite the grip.

Fig 132

Slowly exhaling and using the back muscles, I rotate the drawing shoulder whilst the elbow is brought back through a descending and slightly oblique arc with the drawing forces emanating from the lower area of the *latissimus dorsi*.

Fig 133

The drawing hand guides the release aid down past the face so that the string comes to the side of the chin with the kisser located in the corner of my mouth.

Fig 134

While the string is being drawn, the bow is lowered on to aim. As the string comes to my face, its position is adjusted to bring the peep sight into alignment with the eye, the kisser acting as an additional aid to this.

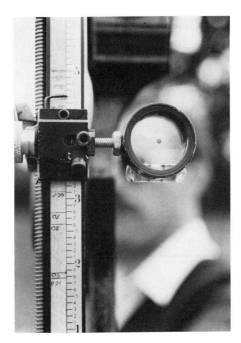

Fig 135

The peep now lines up with the telescopic sight. The final aim and levelling adjustment are made at the same time as the release trigger position is located.

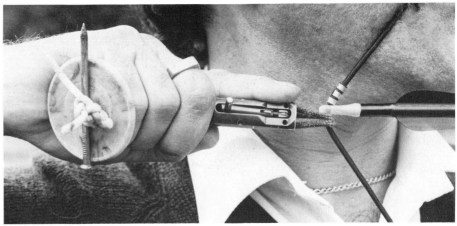

Fig 136

So far the release aid has been on the same plane, with the index finger on top and clear of the trigger.

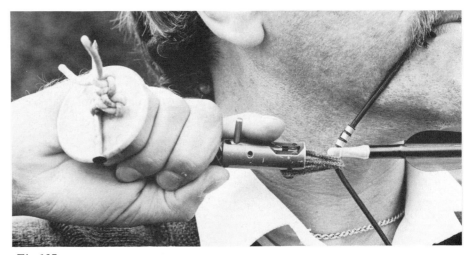

Fig 137

Once located, the hand is turned slightly (say 45 degrees) so that the trigger sticks upward to enable the index fingertip to drop on to it, which gives a smoother, no-punch release when squeezing the trigger off the back.

Fig 138

This is all achieved by first sliding the index fingertip on to the trigger while simultaneously the elbow is pulled back using the same back muscles as before, thus generating a dual-force on the release trigger.

Fig 139

The string is loosed and the elbow continues its oblique arc, downwards and backwards, pulling the release hand into a good natural follow-through. Throughout the drawing and loosing sequence the bow hand remains entirely relaxed.

Naturally, a strong bow arm ensures that the aim is true throughout, even though the release occurs before the brain can compute the deed. The shot is therefore a surprise.

Fig 140

RELEASE AID CONTROL

The worst situation is created when an archer knows exactly when the release is going to happen. This causes punched shots. Control is never as good as with a surprise release. Terry Ragsdale told me that all good releases come as a surprise, whereas those that were deliberately triggered never do. I have always heeded that advice. He and Bob Rhode spent many hours with me on PSE's range when I first became serious about compound shooting. It must have been a frustrating exercise for them, since this was the week prior to the world's biggest indoor tournament at Las Vegas. Hundreds of hours of practice later, I am confident that my consistency in loosing is good enough for Grand Master scores.

Fig 142   Drawing. Forefinger acts as a safety catch over the peg.

Fig 141   Presetting the trigger mechanism.

Fig 143   Peep, telescopic sight and target brought into alignment.

Fig 144   Forefinger drops on to trigger, hand rotates and back tension is increased.

Fig 145   The shot 'breaks' without conscious trigger control.

Fig 146   Follow-through.

ATTENTION TO DETAIL

The Complete Shot Process

Most shooting is all about consistency. At the highest levels of archery, attention to the finest detail produces those vital few extra points. Sequence of events is most important: the foundation of good technique is repetition. Displace any action within that sequence, and the shot goes wrong. For example, say you break down your shot into six distinct stages. Should they lose numerical order and run instead as 1,2,5,4,3,6, then this obvious error will reflect in your performance. Mostly the differences are only detectable by top archers who have perfected their style to a minute degree; but it could mean becoming champion, or not.

We all have off-days when we allow distractions to spoil our concentration which in turn upsets the sequence. The less prone you are to distraction, the greater an archer you will become. One of the worst distractions is weather, which affects even the world champions. The more quickly you acclimatise and learn to read the conditions, the fewer points are lost. Some of my best Master Bowman scores were shot in very peculiar weather; yet there were a couple of bad scores in reasonably good conditions. You must be philosophical and accept good and bad days, but you should be determined to minimise the bad days whatever the conditions and circumstances might be. It is a question of not allowing distractions to break your shooting and mental sequences.

Fig 147

Fig 148

Fig 149

Fig 150

Fig 151

Fig 152

TRAINING

Mental Rehearsal

One way of training to keep my concentration during the shoot is mentally making the shot from approach to the line to follow-through. This mental rehearsal can be done at any time and has helped me shoot better than average by making me intimately aware of my style so that I can detect any break in the sequence. It takes a long time to perfect, but I did it with my recurve as well as my compound. I shoot the shot mentally before I actually make it, so that as I go through the procedure I know if the order is correct. As I come on to aim I think of nothing, but direct all my concentration on the centre of the gold and to feeling the shot. If the feel is wrong, I stop, come down and start again.

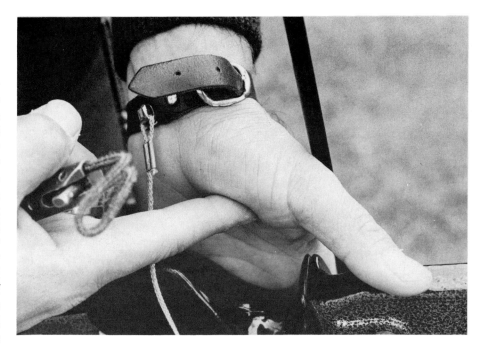

Fig 153   Pressure point.

Training Programmes

During the summer when I practise, I work on one thing in a session. It may be bow tuning, hand position, releasing or whatever. Should it be necessary to work on style changes or to reinforce a particular aspect of style, I shoot at 10 yards at a bare boss or may even blind-loose at 5 yards. Blind-loosing is probably the most relaxing and positive way to learn a shooting skill, because when the eyes are closed the brain is put into neutral and the shot can be felt without any visual distractions to fog the issue. It tells me all I need to know to detect the problem and put it right. I use the system a great deal

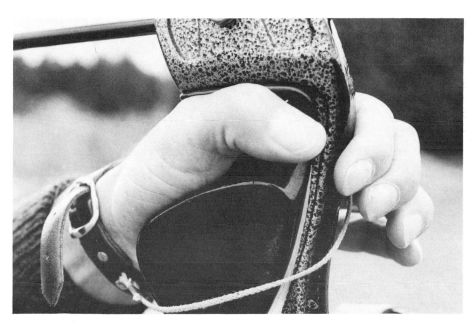

Fig 154   Relaxed grip during draw.

Fig 155   Full draw.

Fig 156   Relaxation continues while the arrow escapes.

when coaching others no matter what their standard if I think they can benefit from it.

At the height of the season I practise two or three times a week, work and family commitments permitting. Unless working on something specific, however, I get bored with aimless practice and prefer competition to keep the adrenalin racing. I am only motivated when competing. This lack of dedication to practice has probably held me back from greater things. In 1986 I won seven county titles, but my best scores were still after a period of extra training. I always have a break from shooting between November and February to rest the body and recharge my batteries. I am not bothered about indoor scores because they mean nothing to me personally. Yorks and FITAs sort the men out from the boys, I think. During this rest period I watch my diet to keep my weight stable, and work with light weights to keep the muscles toned. I accelerate the fitness training between February and March so that I can peak in June, July and August and coast through until September – which brings me through to field shoots in autumn.

Good shooting is also aggressive – though not outwardly so, and certainly not directed at other archers. We must learn to control aggression so that it works for us. Provided we maintain the enjoyment angle, competitive urge and self-motivation will not destroy us when things go wrong. Paradoxically perhaps, we should call it 'passive aggression'. At the end of the day, after all the preparation and training, when asked why I am a better than average archer, I think the reason is willingness to experiment coupled with confidence in my ability and determination to win whilst not losing the enjoyment factor. If I did not enjoy archery, I would stop shooting.

Fig 157   Predraw.

Fig 158   Elbow moves through arc to create back tension as required.

Fig 159   Full draw.

Fig 160   Follow-through.

ATTITUDES

I thrive on competition. I hate losing and love to see my name at the top of the leader board. High class competition is a spur to shooting better. I prefer to let the others worry about what is going on; after all, I am competing only against myself. If I am satisfied with my own performance, that is all that counts. I have no mentor other than myself, and I am a hard taskmaster. You should never mind being beaten by a better archer so long as you shot well; similarly it is a hollow victory if you win against competitors who are not in your league. This is why I set myself a score standard and don't consider what the rest are doing. It may sound blasé, but it works.

Fig 161

Fig 162

Fig 163

Fig 164

Fig 165

EQUIPMENT

Although I started playing with compounds in 1977 and PSE gave me formal training with the bows in 1980, it was not until 1983 that I started to shoot them seriously and realised that to shoot top scores I needed a bow heavier than 46lb peak weight. In 1983 I switched to 58lb, and put 150 points on my FITAs straight away. I never looked back, and was one of only three male archers to qualify for the newly introduced compound Master Bowman award in 1984.

For the past three years I have shot a PSE Laser Magnum Elite set at 54lb on the longest cable slot to give a draw length of 30in. The cable guard is mounted on the upper position and the sight is a Killian Chek-It with a 0.5 diopter ($2\times$ magnification) Pro Scope. I make my own strings from Dacron B50 with monofilament served centres. The nocking point is three Nok Sets above the arrow. A large kisser goes on the top section of the string, along with a Zero peep sight attached to a piece of rubber tube. Bow limbs are set with $\frac{1}{8}$in positive tiller. The stabiliser system is a 6in 'K' V-bar with a 30in long rod and 10in twins, all of them Pro Shop carbons.

I prefer to shoot off a springy rest with a 20oz pressure rather than off a flipper and button. Too many things can go wrong with the latter. The latest shoot-through types bear thinking about because they have a similar effect to a springy but in a different plane. For tuning, I use the often quoted European walk-back

Fig 166   PSE Laser Magnum and stabiliser system.

method but with fletched arrows only and tested from 5 to 60 yards with the help of two bosses. I used an unfletched shaft beforehand to check the nocking height. When tuning I shoot six arrows at each distance and plot a line through the centre of each group, which allows for the occasional poor shot and is therefore more accurate than the single arrow technique.

Generally I prefer a bow that is not too light and which balances well with the stabilisers. Unfortunately, PSE have discontinued the Magnum, thus leaving a gap in the market. However, I am about to test the new Grand Master Elite made by Merlin Bows UK Limited. During early field tests, the bow proved to be of great promise. Although it weighs

Fig 167   The Bjorn nocks are simply pressed on to the arrow shaft.

7½lb with Merlin sight, scope, cable guard and 30in long rod, the Grand Master Elite is very stable in-hand, has minimal torque on loose and sits comfortably in the hand with a standard low grip. It is very easy to tune and more versatile than most. If it continues to shoot well for me – fast, accurate and responsive to my style – I'll probably switch to it.

I have been shooting 2014 X7s with 9 per cent NIBB points, PSE ProFletch PF230 vanes and Bjorn nocks, but Merlin assure me that if I change to their bow, I'll need 1914 X7s instead. Whatever happens, I shall stick with my system of not gluing on the nocks because it enables me to change if I find somebody else on my target shooting the same colours. Eleven years ago, when I began this practice, I was scorned by everyone; now it seems to be common. My fletching angle is no more than one degree right-hand spiral. Although I like the lightness of ProFletch, I am experimenting with FlexFletch because of their high definition colour range. My arrows also carry FITA field numbering decals. I think it is essential that all good archers personally maintain their equipment because it gives them greater understanding of their archery.

Releases

Having shot many release aids (including Fletchmatic TR and FF, HotShot, Failsafe, Lyons, Stanislawski and American Hunter) I still go back to my trusted Fletchmatic palm draw release which has been adapted with a 3in nail and piece of hosepipe! Every time I try another type, the first score is good but the rest are disastrous. The Fletchmatic has given me all my best scores over the past four years and fits like a favourite pair of slippers.

SHOOTING THE COMPOUND

What to Look for

When an archer asks what he needs to change from recurve to compound, several points have to be established:

1. True draw length.
2. What weight can he manage at peak?
3. Does he wish to shoot limited or unlimited style?
4. Does he have a sighting impediment?
5. Is his current equipment reusable or adaptable?
6. How much can he afford?
7. Product preferences.

Fig 168   Bow feels stiffer than a recurve at predraw.

Draw length is the most important factor, because without the right specification two undesirable situations arise: arrows that are too short can be dangerous; if they are too long, the dead weight causes bad matching and unnecessary loss of sight mark. To establish the correct draw length, watch the archer draw his recurve with a measuring arrow and correct any faults due to bad posture and inefficient drawing technique. It is pointless going further until defects such as these are identified.

Then, using the correct elevated draw-up method, measure the draw length to the back of the bow when the string has been pulled to the side of the mouth (but still kept in contact with the nose). This is a baseline from which to select a compound

Fig 169   Peak draw weight occurs early.

Fig 170   Weight falls off at full draw, usually by 50 per cent.

Fig 171   Eccentric wheels with draw length adjustment slots.

bow. The bow should reach that dimension with the cables set in the centre slots of the eccentric wheels.

From brace height to half-way through the draw, a compound bow's draw weight increases sharply before falling by approximately 50 per cent when holding length is reached. An elevated draw more evenly distributes the effort required and greatly assists in an archer's first attempts to draw. Set the bow to between 45 and 50lb for men; those for ladies and juniors are set to 30–35lb peak weight depending on their size. As a starting point, peak weight should be no less than the recurve holding weight, and invariably ends up about 5lb more for men and 2–3lb more for women. You can tell whether the bow is too heavy by watching the reaction of the archer's bow shoulder when peak weight occurs and its position thereafter.

Before checking the final draw length, the archer must familiarise himself with the bow by pulling and letting down several times with a clenched grip just to get the feel of the leverage action of the wheels. After that, he uses a release aid (unlimited) or a tab (limited) to draw back comfortably in line, using a side anchor location. When it is settled at full draw, look at the cable exit from the eccentric wheels to see if the bow's draw length setting is indeed correct.

The axle of a compound eccentric wheel is off-centre, and therefore the wheel acts as a lever when pulled around by the string and cable. Using an imaginary line drawn across the wheel's diameter from the centre of the axle hole, place a mark on the rim of the wheel at the point furthest away. This indicates the line of maximum leverage, and is the point at which the cable should exit from the wheel if the draw length is correct for the archer. A draw force curve of the bow would show it to be at maximum let-off at this point, also known as 'in the valley'. The valley is the area of relaxation, usually 50 per cent of peak weight, at the end of the draw. When an archer is learning to shoot a compound, the middle of the valley is the point most favoured for consistency. Personally, I prefer to shoot from the back of the valley nearer the slope, but not on the stops. This is a matter for experimentation, though, as well as of personal preference.

Both wheels must roll over identically to maintain the bow's dynamic balance irrespective of whether you use fingers or a release aid. If you draw up shorter or longer than the bow's settings permit, either the cable slot settings must be changed or the eccentrics should be exchanged for others of larger or smaller diameter. Most wheels have three slots to give three different draw lengths. The centre slot equates with the bow's stated draw length. The inside slot adds an extra one inch; the third slot reduces draw length by one inch from the stated figure. Ideally, a bow should be shot with the cable in the centre-slot, but it will perform well in the other two as well.

Fig 172   Limb tiller, cable exit and wheel synchronisation must be balanced at full draw.

BOW SELECTION

Several things must be considered when selecting a bow besides whether you like the colour and can afford it. First comes the design of the limb, one aspect of which is gauged by its *pre-bend* which is calculated by measuring the limb's static deflection before it is drawn. This should be 2–4in for optimum performance. Less than 2in gives poor performance but long limb life; more than 4in overstresses the limbs at full draw. At full draw, the limb deflection is termed *dynamic deflection*. American experts assure us that 5–6in is the optimum.

Two basic types of limb are available: wood and glass laminated as in recurve bows; and the more recent carbon graphite and glassfibre mixed in a solid compressed limb. The latter is obviously lighter and faster, but the traditional type is definitely more stable in my opinion. It also seems sweeter to draw and shoot, and in my experience as a dealer is more reliable and less vulnerable to extremes of temperature. Price reflects these differences: laminated limbs are £60–150 more expensive on average. The customer must decide which feels better and shoots more smoothly. My advice is to go for the stability of the laminated limb, be it straight or recurved.

Handle geometry is less critical than limb design but is still important when looking for top scores. A riser with too great a deflex angle creates a high brace height and gives poor performance. The straighter the riser the better, because pre-

Fig 173 Limb construction affects the feel of the bow during release and follow-through.

bend then governs brace height, which makes the bow efficient when working in the desirable 2–4in band. One recently introduced bow, the Oneida Eagle, has a reflex type handle which offers less inertia around the grip but is coupled to a complex internal cam system and hinged recurve limb tips. Although very efficient, it is ridiculously expensive in Britain. Preformed recurve compound limbs are the design of the future and have already collected an impressive list of record scores. Such limbs are featured on the Merlin Grand Master.

Tying up Loose Ends

Whatever bow is decided upon, it must balance in-hand with the barest stabilisation and feel good to shoot. Even though many prefer the V-bar set-up or the American Dream range of twin stabiliser mountings, generally I suggest a simple carbon long rod 30–36in long. Once the selection is made, fit the cable guard (in the high position if there is a choice) then customise the weights and tiller to suit the shooting style. Arrow rest and pressure button – or springy rest – nocking point, peep sight and kisser are then fitted. Set the bow just over centre-shot as a prelude to tuning, with $\frac{1}{8}$in tiller for unlimited and $\frac{1}{4}$in for limited style. However, this may need altering to suit the individual.

Arrow Matching

Invariably most new compound shooters end up with a draw weight

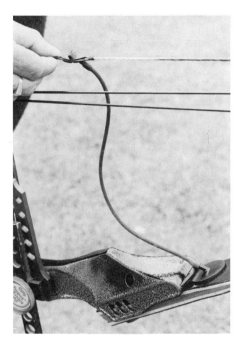

Fig 174 Peep sight and alignment device.

Fig 175 Telescopic sights.

Fig 176 Plain aperture and levelling bubble.

Fig 177 Flipper and pressure button (left) for finger shooting. A springy rest suits the release aid.

compatible with their existing arrows, but may find them too short. For example, an archer shooting a recurve of 42lb on the fingers at 29in will be able to use a 55lb, 50 per cent let-off compound, which calls for the same spine rating shafts as before. Be guided by the Easton matrix which allows for compounds of various let-offs. I must stress, though, that the charts are only a guide, and that the majority of compounds will shoot a variety of shafts if they are tuned accordingly. One of the most versatile is the X7 1914 which appears to be the most popular of all. You should also be aware of new developments in carbon-reinforced resin arrows that offer strength and lower surface friction, even if no advantage is gained from their lightness.

Release Aids

A novice fresh from a beginner's course who chooses a compound straight away should use a finger tab until he has mastered the basic art of shooting. However, if an experienced archer changes to a compound there is no reason why he should not start with a mechanical release aid: whichever feels most comfortable in-hand and inspires confidence is best. The latest Jim Fletcher creations, Fletchmatic TR and FF are so fast that a novice would not cope with them, but the original palm draw model or the Stuart HotShot are very simple to control. Gourley's Fail-safes are perhaps the safest of all, but so fiddly that they deter the beginner. Some can manage the Fletchmatic with a wrist sling (also known as a concho design), but it is not as safe as the palm draw. These brands are the most popular by far and are all adjustable for sensitivity. Target releases are lighter than hunting models. Always start with a medium setting to get the feel of it.

Peep Sights, Scopes and Bubbles

Because of its no-fuss automatic line-up due to the rubber band attachment, Fine Line's Zero Peep is the best to start with. The standard TruPeep and PaPeep that are independently fitted to the string are excellent, but must be set at the right angle so that they twist into alignment at full draw. All peeps should be hooded against sun glare, and the aperture must be compatible with the magnification of your scope.

Depending on your eyesight and the peep aperture, you can have anything from 2 to 6$\times$ magnification on your telescopic sight lens. I usually recommend 2$\times$ or 3$\times$ (0.5 or 0.75 diopter) for beginners with normal vision. Most scopes and pins are threaded 8/32in and fit the latest Arten, Merlin and 'K' sights, plus any that are made in America. All should be fitted with a spirit level as an additional aid. Levels are allowed in the limited class provided there is a standard ring or pin element in the sight, not a magnifier. As soon as either a scope or a release is used, the outfit is classed as unlimited. Whatever sight is mounted, it must be perfectly aligned in both horizontal and vertical planes. Using a door frame that is truly upright, a plumb line or a spirit level, this can be achieved satisfactorily. You may need to pack out the sight mounting block.

Button or Springy Rest

My maxim has always been that if you shoot with fingers, use a pressure button and flip rest. With a release, use a springy rest instead. The latest rests primarily intended for release shooting are shoot-through or drop-away types which allow for zero divergence of the arrow; in other words, shooting right on centre with minimum paradox. They also allow a right-hand bow to be shot left-handed and still get perfect tuning. More data is required to convince me. Any rest that offers the least resistance to the arrow and causes no deflection is the best one; but trial and error is the only way to establish which is best for you personally. All that remains is to go out and shoot. Go for gold. Be positive, but don't expect miracles overnight. Be prepared to work long and hard.

JOHN HOLDEN

112 pages   257 × 210mm

100 photographs   0 946284 31 8

A comprehensive and fully illustrated study of archery techniques and practice from Britain's outstanding archer.

120 pages   246 × 189mm

97 photographs   1 85223 010 X

A detailed survey of archery equipment, covering tournament, field and hunting tackle, with advice on all aspects from selection and tuning to the principles of bow and arrow performance.